THE BOAT CONTEST

Featuring Aesop's The Lion and The Mouse

LAMB CHOP'S FABLES

THE BOAT CONTEST

featuring

AESOP'S
The Lion and the Mouse

by

SHARI LEWIS

TIME
LIFE
CUSTOM
PUBLISHING

For Matthew, Jessica, Squeezy and Rachel

○○○○○

WITH A DEEP AND GRATEFUL BOW TO LAN O'KUN

TIME-LIFE CUSTOM PUBLISHING

VICE PRESIDENT AND PUBLISHER: Susan J. Maruyama

Production Manager: Prudence G. Harris

Editor: Blaine Marshall

Operations Manager: Phyllis A. Gardner

Promotions Manager: Becky Wheeler

Associate Promotions Manager: Gary Stoiber

Retail Sales Manager: Lorna Milkovich

Acknowledgements: Dana Coleman • Patricia Loushine

Becky Merson • Tracey Warner

Time-Life Books
is a division of Time Life Incorporated.,

TIME-LIFE BOOKS
PRESIDENT: John Hall

Illustrations by MANNY CAMPANA
and
JEAN PIDGEON (fable)

○○○○○

Produced by Lucas-Evans Books, Inc.
Designed by Alfred Giuliani
Cover Design by Nina Bridges

Library of Congress Cataloging-in-Publication Data
Lewis, Shari.
The boat contest: featuring Aesop's The lion and the mouse / written by Shari Lewis.
p. cm.-(Lamb Chop's fables)
Summary: Lamb Chop learns an important lesson in life after hearing Aesop's fable "The Lion and the Mouse."
ISBN 0-8094-7446-8 : $8.95 ($11.95 Can.)
[1. Conduct of life-Fiction. 2. Contests-Fiction. 3. Fables.]
I. Aesop. II. Lion and the mouse. III. Title. IV. Series: Lewis, Shari. Lamb Chop's fables.
PZ7.L5879Bo 1993
[E]-dc20
93-3768
CIP
AC

It was Lamb Chop who discovered the little pond in the park.

MODEL
BOAT
BUILDING
CONTEST.
BUILD
THE BEST
BOAT!

She and Charlie Horse loved to watch the big kids
sail their boats on the water.
One day a sign was posted on a tree. Charlie read
it out loud: "MODEL BOAT BUILDING CONTEST.
BUILD THE BEST BOAT!"

"I bet I could build the best boat," bragged Charlie Horse.

"Me, too. I could too!" insisted Lamb Chop.

Everybody laughed.

"They're laughing at you," Charlie said to Lamb Chop. "This contest is for us older kids."

"They're laughing at you, too, Charlie," said Lamb Chop.

Shari took them to the harbor to look at the big boats. Some boats were tied to the dock. Larger ones sailed in the deeper water.

"Why does that big boat have a baby boat on a leash?" asked Lamb Chop.

"So that people can row from their big boat to the shore," answered Charlie Horse.

When they went to the craft shop, Lamb Chop chose a simple kit that could be made into a little rowboat.

Charlie picked a very difficult boat model, with lots of parts to be put together.

"Won't that be too hard to build?" asked Lamb Chop.

"For you," answered Charlie Horse. "But not for me. I'm going to win that contest!"

But Charlie Horse did have a hard time building his boat.

"So many little pieces," he said. "I wonder if I really can build a better boat than all those other kids."

"Don't worry about the other kids," said Shari. "Just enjoy doing the best you can."

Lamb Chop's rowboat was easy to put together, and she finished it quickly.
"Look what I made," she said proudly.

Charlie Horse snapped, "Your boat's too small, just like you. You can't win."

And now, setting her little boat beside his big ship, Lamb Chop felt foolish.

"Charlie Horse is right," she thought to herself. "I'm just too little."

The day before the contest, Charlie had still not finished.

"Now can I help you?" offered Lamb Chop.

"How could *you* help me?" answered Charlie Horse.

"I'm your friend, Charlie," said Lamb Chop. "That's what friends are for."

But Charlie Horse just snickered and said, "You're too little to really be my friend."

Lamb Chop climbed into Shari's lap.

"How about a story?" asked Shari, putting aside her newspaper.

Lamb Chop snuggled closer.

"I guess that means yes," said Shari. "Okay, here's the Aesop fable called "The Lion and the Mouse."

"Aesop?" asked Lamb Chop.

"He made up this story," answered Shari.

Aesop Says:

It happened once upon a time, so the story goes.
A sleeping lion felt somebody run across his nose.
His eyes popped open and he snarled, "Who on earth would dare
To wake me from my sleep?" He saw a mouse was standing there.

The lion growled, "Look what you've done, you clumsy little thing! Your tiny feet have run across the nostrils of a king!"

The mighty lion roared, in a terrifying way.
He told the frightened mouse, "I'm going to eat you up today!"

The mouse said, "Sir, I'd hardly make a satisfying chew,
For someone who's as wonderfully big and strong as you.
I'm sorry I awakened you, but if you set me free,
Why, some day I'll do something nice for you.
Just wait and see!

Please let me go. You never know just how tomorrow will end.
And who can tell what use a mouse could be, especially to a friend."

The lion was so amused that he finally agreed.
And the mouse ran far away, the minute he was freed.
You should have seen that tiny creature scamper out of sight!
But do you know, the day arrived when the mouse proved that he was right.

For though the lion was big and strong, as strong as you can get,
He got himself entangled in the ropes of a hunter's net.
He twisted and he turned, and the hunter heard him roar.
But the King of Beasts could not escape, since that's what nets are for!

The lion roared again, and the distant hunter cheered.
Then right beside the helpless beast, a tiny mouse appeared.
The lion recognized the mouse, who smiled and said, "It's me!
Be patient, and before the hunter comes, I'll set you free."

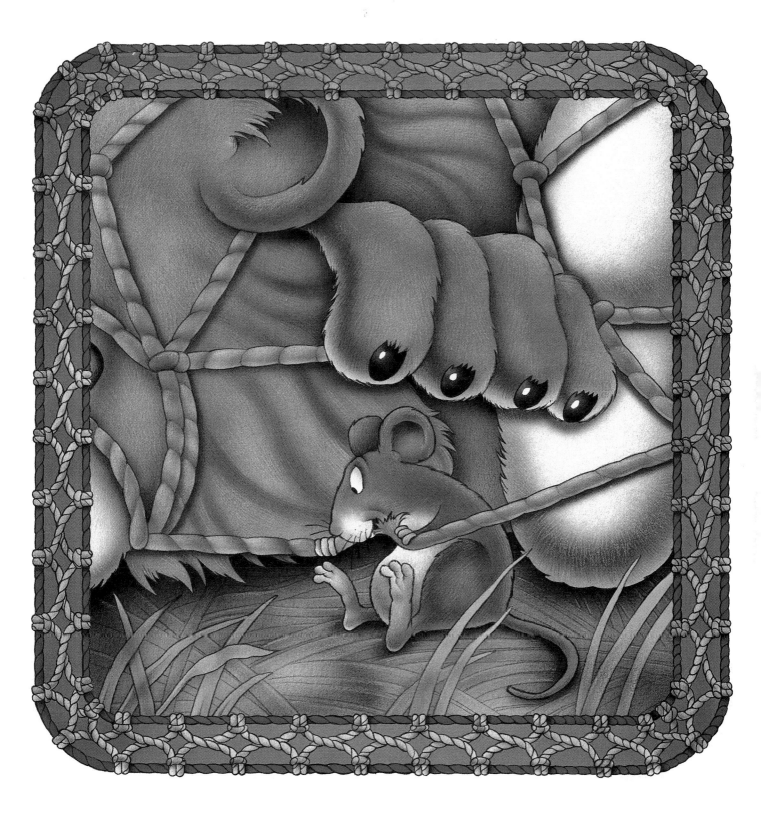

So one by one, between his teeth, the ropes began to fray,
AND SUDDENLY WITH A SNAP THEY BROKE—and the lion got away!
Which only proves that the smallest mouse can sometimes save the day.

Here's the moral of this story—
Which is always at the end—
NOBODY IS TOO SMALL TO HELP
WHEN SOMEONE NEEDS A FRIEND.

The day of the contest arrived. There were lots of children and lots of boats.
Charlie Horse set his boat into the water.

"Oh, no!" whispered Charlie Horse. "That girl built the same model as mine. Why would the judges pick my boat as the best when hers is no different?"

Lamb Chop thought for a moment. Then she bent down and began to pull a shoelace from Charlie's sneaker.

Finally all the boats were in the water. The judges walked 'round and 'round. Last of all they stopped and looked at Charlie's boat.

There was a moment of silence. Then the judges smiled and said, "That's the winner. Such a clever idea."

Of all the boats sailing on the pond, only Charlie's had a little rowboat trailing behind it.

Everyone applauded when Charlie Horse got the prize. As he shook the judge's hand, Charlie said, "Thank you. But I want to share this prize with my good friend, Lamb Chop."

Lamb Chop Says:

"You may be little, but don't ever think little of yourself. Even the smallest of us can do big things!"